MY ART BOOK

Animals

A DORLING KINDERSLEY BOOK

DK

LONDON, NEW YORK, MUNICH,
MELBOURNE, and DELHI

Project editor Alexander Cox
Senior designer Sonia Moore
Editor Lorrie Mack
Designers Gemma Fletcher, Rosie Levine,
and Lauren Rosier

Photographer Will Heap
Art consultant Ian Chilvers
Picture researcher Jo Walton
Production editor Siu Chan
Production controller Kara Wallace
Jacket designer Rosie Levine
Publishing manager Bridget Giles
Creative director Jane Bull
Category publisher Mary Ling

First published in Great Britain in 2012 by
Dorling Kindersley Limited
80 Strand, London WC2R 0RL

A CIP catalogue record for this book
is available from the British Library.

ISBN: 978-1-40539-148-1

Printed and bound in China
by Hung Hing

Discover more at
www.dk.com

CONTENTS

Have a walk on the wild side of art
and discover these amazing animal
masterpieces inside!

6 Walls of art
- Paints & plaster
- Burial scenes

14 Wooden rhino
- Tin tortoise
- Life drawing

Discover how to paint, sculpt,

28 Horse power
- Drawing horses
- Beasts of beauty

34 Holy Symbol
- Tiger model
- Starry stripes

20 Mane man
- King of masks
- Touch of genius

44 Living colours
- Wax elephants
- Curves & lines

engrave, draw, model, and create amazing animal art!

58 Fish and shapes
- Crab collage
- Master's animals

64 Cool cats
- Inky dogs
- Wild ideas

50 Klee colour
- Stencil birds
- Fancy flyers

70 Animals for all
- Monkey on a wire
- Animal shapes

Scale

In order to show how large or small a piece of art is we have compared it to this hand or child.

The child is 110 cm (43 in) tall.

The hand is 12 cm (5 in) high.

78 Glossary and Index

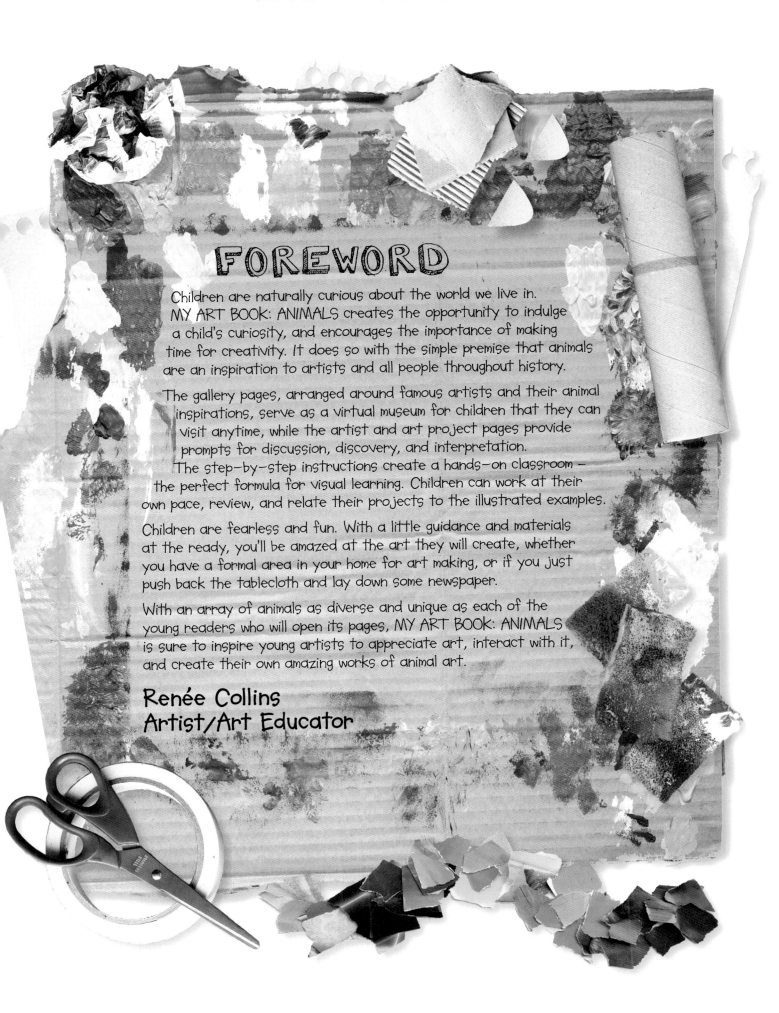

FOREWORD

Children are naturally curious about the world we live in.
MY ART BOOK: ANIMALS creates the opportunity to indulge
a child's curiosity, and encourages the importance of making
time for creativity. It does so with the simple premise that animals
are an inspiration to artists and all people throughout history.

The gallery pages, arranged around famous artists and their animal
inspirations, serve as a virtual museum for children that they can
visit anytime, while the artist and art project pages provide
prompts for discussion, discovery, and interpretation.
The step-by-step instructions create a hands-on classroom –
the perfect formula for visual learning. Children can work at their
own pace, review, and relate their projects to the illustrated examples.

Children are fearless and fun. With a little guidance and materials
at the ready, you'll be amazed at the art they will create, whether
you have a formal area in your home for art making, or if you just
push back the tablecloth and lay down some newspaper.

With an array of animals as diverse and unique as each of the
young readers who will open its pages, MY ART BOOK: ANIMALS
is sure to inspire young artists to appreciate art, interact with it,
and create their own amazing works of animal art.

Renée Collins
Artist/Art Educator

Walls of art

THE ANCIENT EGYPTIANS painted pictures on the interior walls of tombs. They surrounded the dead with familiar scenes to guide and help them in the afterlife. This fresco shows the cattle of Egyptian nobleman Nebamun being presented for inspection.

The hieroglyphs behind the farmers tell the story of how the farmers argued as they moved through the queue.

The cattle are shown in five layers and the Egyptian artists use different colours to separate the images.

Cattle Brought For Inspection
Unknown artist, **c.1350 BCE,**
wall painting (fresco)

The fresco is this **big!**

Cats were originally
wild animals, but were
domesticated by the
ancient Egyptians.

Egypt and animals

The cat was a sacred animal to the ancient Egyptians. They worshipped it because of its skill at killing vermin, such as rats and snakes. The Egyptians respected their cats so much that families would mummify their favourite animals after they died.

Draw like an Egyptian

The ancient Egyptian artists were more interested in clarity than accuracy. They drew the human body facing forward, but the head in side view. Animals were drawn side on and some features, such as eyes, were made larger to give the drawings more impact.

This artwork is one of a few fragments that remain from the tomb of Nebamun. The paint has survived for thousands of years in Egypt's dry climate.

The Egyptians also worshipped animal-headed gods. These included, lions, hawks, crocodiles, and even a frog.

PAINTS & PLASTER

! Avoid skin contact when handling plaster.

You will need:

Light plaster
Mixing bowls
A jar of water
Foil container
Wooden spoon
Colour pastels
Sandwich bags
Paint brushes

A foil container is essential (plastic containers may melt).

Making plaster

This project uses light plaster, which is tricky to mix and must be handled with care, so ask an adult to help and avoid skin contact with the plaster. Light plaster dries very quickly, so it's a good idea to get everything ready before you begin.

1 Choose the colours you want to use on your fresco. Place each pastel in a separate bag and carefully crush the pastels with a wooden spoon.

2 Read the mixing and safety instructions on the back of the light plaster and ask an adult to carefully mix the required amount with water.

3 As the plaster is mixed, pour in the crushed pastel of your chosen background colour and stir it into the plaster mix.

4 After the pastel and plaster has been mixed, carefully pour it into the foil tray and smooth the top with the back of a spoon. You can sink a knotted piece of string into the wet plaster so you can hang up your fresco once it's finished.

5 While the plaster dries make sure you have all your pastels crushed, and pour a couple of spoonfuls of plaster into the jar of water.

6 Pour your crushed pastels into separate bowls and mix the powdered pastel with some of the plaster water to make a wet paste.

7 Using your chosen colour, paint the outline of your animal. You can add more water to the pastel paste if it gets too dry.

8 Build up the colours on your fresco one by one. The pastel paint will dry slowly, so be careful not to smudge or mix the colours.

Finishing touches

To make your fresco look like it's been discovered inside an Egyptian tomb, add details like hieroglyphs and Egyptian patterns.

BURIAL SCENES

In ancient Egypt, fine tomb frescoes honoured important people after their death.

Tomb of Tutankhamun

This baboon detail comes from one of the many animal scenes in the tomb of the famous boy Pharoah.

Tomb of Menna

Menna was a scribe (clerk) to Tuthmoses IV, so he was important enough to have a grand tomb adorned with images like this fishing scene.

Tomb of Nefermaat

This is part of a long thin image showing six geese in all. They are so finely painted that experts think Nefermaat must have been royal.

Tomb of Sennedjem

Here, Sennedjem is using two dappled (spotty) oxen to sow grain in the blessed fields of the afterlife.

Tomb of Nekhtamun

Ra, the sun god, is shown in the form of a cat, killing the serpent god Apophis.

Tomb of Sennedjem

The man this tomb was made for was not royal, but it is extremely fine. Here the god Isis (below), disguised as a falcon, stands guard.

Wooden rhino

Rhinoceros
by Albrecht Dürer, **1515**,
print from woodcut

ALBRECHT DÜRER (1471–1528) was a German painter and printmaker. His prints were produced in large numbers spreading his fame across Europe.

The print is this **big!**

Can you spot the differences between Dürer's *Rhinoceros* and a real rhinoceros?

Self Portrait
Albrecht Dürer, 1500

Wood Cutter

Dürer was one of the main artists of the Northern Renaissance era. Many of his famous artworks are woodcuts. These were made by carving the image onto the surface of a smooth wooden block. The block was then coated in ink so a print on paper could be made.

Rhinoceros sighting

Dürer never actually saw a real rhinoceros; he created his *Rhinoceros* woodcut from a written description and an illustration of the first rhinoceros seen in Europe for about one thousand years.

An Indian Rhinoceros

Creative anatomy

Dürer's woodcut of the rhinoceros remained the main reference illustration for hundreds of years, even though the image was more fanciful creation than accurate animal art.
Dürer's *Rhinoceros* has tortoiseshell armour that seems to be riveted in place, scaly legs, and an extra horn on its back.

Dürer gave his rhinoceros scales like a lizard.

Dürer took inspiration from the world around him, and he added a kind of "gorget" to his rhinoceros. This was a piece of neck armour worn by knights of the period.

Artist

TIN TORTOISE

You will need:

Foil tray
Masking tape
Scissors
Tracing paper
Pens
Wooden skewer
Black paint and brush

1 Find an image of a tortoise and using tracing paper, trace the outline of the animal.

2 Cut the foil tray so it's the same size as your traced tortoise. Tape the tracing paper securely to the foil.

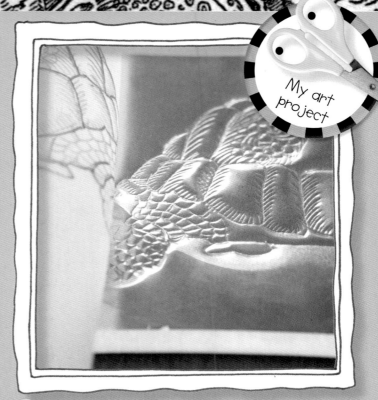

3 Using a black pen, press firmly and draw over the outline of the tortoise. With a different colour pen, draw detail onto the tortoise shell, feet, and head.

4 Every now and again check the foil to see how your tin tortoise is looking. Be careful not to move the tracing paper or the foil out of place.

5 Once you have filled in all the detail, remove the tracing paper and you have a cool engraving of a tin tortoise!

Why not trace Dürer's Rhinceros and turn it into a tin engraving!

Frame your finished piece or stick it onto a notebook to make a shiny cover.

As a finishing touch, you can paint around your tin engraving and scratch patterns into the paint with a wooden skewer.

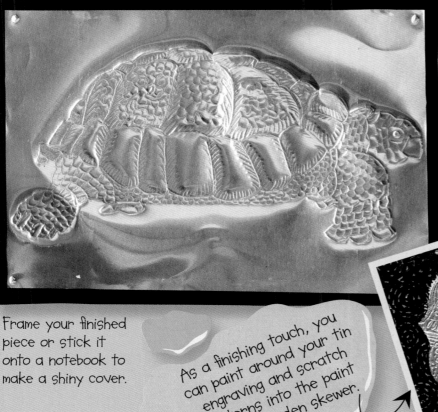

LIFE DRAWING

Dürer was the first great artist to be fascinated by the whole animal kingdom.

A Young Hare 1502

This little animal looks alert, as if it could jump up at any second, but experts think Dürer painted it from a stuffed model.

The Little Owl 1508

Look at the bottom of this picture, on the left – can you find Dürer's special monogram, or signature? It's a little "D" inside a big "A".

Wing of a Roller 1512

When Dürer was alive, lots of new animals and plants were being found all over the world. The bright roller bird whose wing he depicted here was exotic and exciting in 1512.

Squirrels 1512

Dürer painted these hungry nibblers in a type of watercolour called gouache. This is especially thick, so the paper doesn't show through.

Head of a Roe Deer 1514

This small, reddish-brown deer, which is well suited to Germany's cold winters, is still common in Europe and Asia.

Monkey *date unknown*

Experts think Dürer painted this monkey, but they're not absolutely sure, so they say it's "attributed" to him.

Mane man

PETER PAUL RUBENS (1577-1640) was known as the "prince of painters and painter of princes". He was the most famous, versatile, and successful artist of his time.

Daniel in the Lions' Den by Peter Paul Rubens, **1615**, oil on canvas

The big picture

Daniel was counsellor to King Darius. The king's other ministers were jealous, and had Daniel locked in a lions' den. The next morning, when Darius moved the entrance stone, he found Daniel safe, and giving thanks to God.

The painting is this **big!**

Most of the things in this picture are brown – such as the fur on the animals, and the large areas of rock. Against all this brown, Daniel's pale skin and red robe stand out, so you look at him first.

Perfect practice

Before they produce oil paintings, many artists make drawings of what they want to show. Rubens did this drawing of a lioness in coloured chalks – can you see the finished animal in his painting?

Royal Rubens

Named after two saints, Peter Paul Rubens was born in Siegen (Germany), but lived most of his life in Flanders (Belgium). A scholar who spoke several languages, he painted pictures for royal and noble families across Europe. Rubens loved ancient sculpture, and he exchanged a number of his works for a collection of Roman statues.

Self Portrait
Peter Paul Rubens, 1623

KING OF MASKS

You will need:
Cardboard
Chalk
Masking tape
Scissors
Paper bags and envelopes
PVA glue
Paint brush and paints

1 Make sure your piece of cardboard is big enough to cover your face and sketch a lion's face in chalk.

2 Use a paper bag or envelope to make a nose. You can pad it out with scrap paper.

3 Carefully, cut out your lion's face and secure the lion's nose using strips of masking tape.

4 Fold some paper bags into thirds lengthways, then fold them into a concertina shape. Cut along the folds to create strips, leaving a few centimetres (inches) uncut at the top.

5 To make the mane curly, wrap the strips around a paint brush then unwind. For effect, curl the top layer more than the bottom layer.

6 To make the lion's ears, cut large circles out of a paper bag. Hold the bottom of the circle and pinch it together, as shown.

23

7 Position the ears on your mask and glue in place. You can also use masking tape to make sure they are securely attached.

8 To make your head band, cut some cardboard into long strips. Wrap the head band around your head to make sure it fits then tape it to the mask. The support strip sits on top of your head.

9 You can now add your mane to your mask. Repeat steps 4 and 5 so you have lots of curly mane sections and glue them to the inside of the mask.

10 Use yellow, orange, and red to paint the lion's face. Then use black paint to emphasise the eyes, nose, and mouth.

Cover the inside of the mask with an oval piece of card, so you don't scratch your face on the mane.

Make two eye holes in the mask by pushing a sharp pencil through the mask into a lump of sticky tack beneath.

Why not paint some yellow detail on the ends of the curly mane. You are now ready to show off your new mask... GROWL!

TOUCH OF GENIUS

Rubens treated every subject brilliantly – his animals look as if they might come alive.

Marriage of Henri IV and Marie de Médicis c1623

These cherub-bearing lions suggest power and strength. They also make a visual joke on "Lyon" in France, which is where the king and queen first met.

Can you find the mouse?

This story (below right) just might be true – when restorers cleaned the picture recently, they found overpainting on the mouse. They removed it!

The Lion and the Mouse c1620

Rubens created this scene with his friend Frans Snyders. It once hung in the country house of Winston Churchill, a keen amateur artist – according to one story, he couldn't see the mouse clearly, so he touched it up!

Tiger Hunt *c*1617

Rubens' studio produced lots of enormous, crowded hunting scenes – this one is more than 3m (9ft) wide! Rubens could never have seen some of the exotic animals he painted, so he probably worked from stuffed models.

Parrot *c*1630

Rubens had lots of other artists working for him. Experts think one of them painted this with Rubens' guidance.

Portrait of Giovanni Carlo Doria on Horseback *c*1606

Doria was an important Italian nobleman. To reflect his great power and influence, Rubens painted him on a charging steed.

Horse power

ALTHOUGH HE BEGAN his career producing portraits of people, George Stubbs (1724-1806) is now famous as the greatest horse painter of all time. This portrait is by Ozias Humphry.

Life studies

After studying human anatomy (what's inside bodies), Stubbs turned his attention to horses. In 1766, he published his famous book, *The Anatomy of the Horse,* creating all the illustrations himself. He knew horses better than any other artist and painted them with great energy, like the white one shown here. The lion looks a bit lifeless, though – Stubbs probably used the skin trophy from an exotic hunt as his model.

Time to learn

In order to learn all about horses' bodies, Stubbs spent 18 months in the English countryside, drawing as many animals as he could, and cutting up dead ones.

The inspiration for this scene may have been a trip to Morocco, where Stubbs saw a lion attacking a horse. There is also an ancient statue with this theme, which he could have known.

A Horse Frightened by a Lion
by George Stubbs, **1770,**
oil on canvas

The painting is this big!

Wherever the idea came from, Stubbs fell in love with
it – in total, he produced nearly 20 similar pictures.

DRAWING HORSES

You will need:

Black card
Masking tape
Tracing paper
Colour pastels
Pencil
Rubber

A Horse's body

Before you start you need to plan your picture. Have a look at Stubbs' horse and break it down into simple shapes.

The horse's head and neck become rectangles and triangles. The body is a large rectangle with circles at the joints. Use simple lines for the legs.

You can use black paper.

1 Draw the horse shapes straight onto the black card, or tape tracing paper over Stubbs' horse, copy the shapes, and then transfer them onto the card.

2 Using a white pastel and a stronger line, draw the outline of your horse by fleshing out the basic horse shapes.

3 Now fill in the horse using your white pastel. You can always refer back to Stubbs' horse if you need help with the detail.

Use your finger to blend the colours.

4 Use a dark grey or black pastel to add shadows to parts of the horse. Use curving strokes to show the "roundness" of the horse's belly.

As a finishing touch, blend some yellow and brown chalk to create an earth-coloured ground.

31

BEASTS OF BEAUTY

As a painter-scientist, George Stubbs was fascinated by all wild and domestic creatures.

Fanny, a Brown and White Spaniel 1778

John Musters was one of Stubbs' most important patrons (people who commission work). Fanny was the much-loved pet of Musters' wife Sophia.

Cheetah and Stag with Two Indians
*c*1765

This painting illustrates the true story of an aristocrat who ordered his servants to release a wild cat and a stag so he could watch the kill – but the stag escaped!

Warren Hastings on his American Horse 1796

The first Governor-General of India, Hastings was accused of corruption, but was cleared the year before this portrait was painted.

Whistlejacket c1762

This huge portrait of a famous racehorse – nearly 3m (10ft) tall – was done for his owner, the Marquess of Rockingham. Many stories are told about it – in one, the stallion was so disturbed when he saw his own image that he tried to attack it.

Portrait of a Monkey
1799

Stubbs painted this image twice, 25 years apart – this is the last version. Toward the end of his life, he planned a book of pictures comparing the bodies of humans and animals.

Zebra 1763

Today, we know there are several types of zebra. This is a mountain zebra, but it's called just *Zebra* because it was the only one known in Stubbs' time.

Holy symbol

TIPU SULTAN ruled Mysore in India from 1782 to 1799. For him, the tiger was a holy symbol of power over his enemies – he had tiger decorations on his walls, his throne, his weapons, and his soldiers' uniforms. This life-sized figure was made for Tipu Sultan.

Scary toy

Tipu's Tiger is a type of wind-up toy called an *automaton* – there's a handle coming out of the beast's shoulder (see above). When it's turned, the tiger growls and his victim cries out, lifting his hand to his mouth in terror.

The figures themselves were carved from wood, painted, then covered with shiny lacquer for protection.

Tipu's Tiger
maker unknown, **c1790**, *painted wooden toy*

The figure is this **big!**

Movement and music

Also concealed inside the figure is a small pipe organ. During the 1800s, when the automaton lived in the Reading Room of the East India Company Museum, students constantly grumbled when visitors wound it up and played tunes.

Weighted bellows supply wind to the mechanical organ's 18 pipes. These are operated from an ivory keyboard hidden behind a flap in the animal's side (see above).

The figure being savaged by the tiger is clearly European, but experts aren't sure if he's a soldier or an ordinary man. What do you think?

TIGER MODEL

To make the tiger

This will be the tiger's body.

You will need:
1 plastic drink carton
3 kitchen towel rolls
4 plastic forks
Scrap cardboard
1 dome-shaped lid
Newspaper
Scissors
Masking tape

One for the front legs

Two for the back legs

Cut the kitchen towel rolls.

claws

for the tiger's head

cardboard to make the ears

To make the legs you need to turn the kitchen rolls into small tubes. Cut the kitchen roll in half across its width (1), then cut the halves lengthways (2). Now roll the halves into small thin tubes and secure with tape.

1 Cut off the drink carton's handle and top. Stick the dome-shaped lid to the carton. If you don't have a dome-shaped lid, roll up some newspaper into a ball.

2 Secure the lid to the carton with masking tape – this will be the tiger's head. For the nose, tape on a small ball of newspaper, as shown.

3 Draw some ear shapes on your cardboard and cut them out. Pinch the ears and tape them to your tiger's head using some masking tape.

Add claws to the legs by cutting a plastic fork in half and then sliding it into the end of the tube.

4 For the back legs, cut a u-shape into one cardboard tube, as shown, and tape the joint together. Fill the legs with newspaper to make them solid.

5 Attach the rear legs using masking tape. To attach the front legs, cut 1cm (½in) slits into the attaching end and tape onto the carton, as shown.

6 Roll up a long strip of newspaper for the tail and attach it to the carton. To finish, brush on a layer of watered-down PVA glue.

7 Once the PVA glue is dry, you can start painting the tiger. Start with an orange base coat, then add the black tiger stripes.

8 Finally, paint the face detail onto the tiger and give it a big growling mouth and wide scary eyes!

Your finished tiger should look like this.

To make the man

You will need:
1 sweet box
1 aluminium foil roll
2 plastic teaspoons
Bendy drinking straws
1 lemon squeezy bottle
Scrap cardboard
Scissors
Masking tape

Plastic lid for a hat

Head

Body

A tall chocolate box makes a great body.

Bendy straws for the arms

Cut in half to make two legs.

Plastic teaspoons for the feet

9 Cut the handle off the spoon and tape the spoon to the kitchen roll, as shown. Repeat with the other spoon and roll to make two legs with feet.

10 For the arms, tape together about five straws and cut to size. The bendy ends will form the man's elbow joint.

11 Carefully attach the legs and arms to the sweets box body. Tape the lemon squeezy bottle to the top of the sweets box to make the man's head.

12 Cover the whole man with masking tape and paint him with a coat of watered-down PVA glue. Add the hat to the top of the man's head.

13 When the PVA glue is dry, your man is ready to paint. Use a red for the jacket, and paint the trousers black. Remember to paint his shoes and socks.

14 Finally, paint the detail on to the man's scared face. Once the paint is dry you can stick the tiger on top of the man with some glue.

STARRY STRIPES

Tigers, the biggest of all jungle cats, have always attracted the artist's eye.

Tasmanian Tiger #3 1989

American artist William L Hawkins used shiny enamel paints for his bold figures. He worked from pictures in books and magazines.

Tiger 1966

Rosina Becker do Valle didn't start painting until she was in her 40s. Most of her work concentrates on the forests and folk stories of her native Brazil.

Henri Rousseau's Dream Garden 1997

Rousseau was a French painter who featured tigers and jungles in his work. In this picture, artist Frances Anne Bloomfield imagines him in his own fantasy landscape.

Tiger Shaking Head 1996

Odile Kidd was born in southern Africa, and her work concentrates on the area's wildlife. This life-size image brings out the beast's expression and personality.

Digital Origami Tiger 2010

To mark the Chinese year of the tiger, two of these digitally designed figures toured the world. Inspired by origami (oriental paper folding), they were made from lots of different – recyclable – materials.

Tiger (from life) 1886

This print is based on an earlier (1803) silk painting by Japanese artist Kiuho Toyei. At this time, Japanese culture stressed how unimportant humans are, which is why nature subjects were so popular.

Living colours

FRANZ MARC (1880-1916) was a German Expressionist artist. For him, animals represented innocence, and he used bold shapes and bright colours to try to show how they might feel rather than how they look.

The Red Bull
by Franz Marc, **1912,**
watercolour on paper

The painting is this big!

Man of the spirit

Franz Marc was a very religious man, and at one time he wanted to become a priest. He thought people were too worried about money and power, which is why he cared so much for animals. When the First World War broke out, he joined the army, and he later died in the fighting.

"The feel for life in animals made all that was good in me come out." FRANZ MARC

Why do you think Franz Marc painted his bull in such a strong red? It looks very peaceful, but do you think it's in danger?

Can you see the rough texture of the paper through Marc's paint?

Colour signals

Franz Marc usually showed animals in harmony with nature – he thought they were more beautiful and purer than humans. His bright colours had special meaning for him: blue was male and spiritual, yellow was female and gentle, and red was violent and brutal.

Animals, Franz Marc, 1913

WAX ELEPHANTS

You will need:

Paper
Pencil
Wax crayons
Watercolour paints
Paint brushes
A cup of water

1 Using Franz Marc's graphic style as a guide, draw a simple elephant in a jungle setting.

2 With a wax crayon colour of your choice, draw a thick outline around the elephant.

3 Draw thick outlines using different colours around your jungle setting. Add some fine detail to the bark of the trees and leaves of the plants.

4 Once you've drawn all the outlines, use the watercolours to paint inside the shapes. The wax will stop the paint from bleeding outside the shapes.

CURVES & LINES

Some of Marc's animals have natural shapes, and some are made into split-up images.

Foxes 1913

You can clearly see the head of one fox, but the rest of the animals are broken into angular shapes.

Blue Horse 1911

Franz Marc loved blue – he helped to found a group of Expressionist painters called *Der Blaue Reiter* (The Blue Rider).

Black and Blue Fox 1911

Marc believed that each person has the same response to individual colours, so painters can use them to express emotion. Why do you think this fox is blue?

Three Animals (Dog, Fox, Cat) 1912

In this painting, and the one of the tiger (below), you can see Marc's animals just starting to take on geometric shapes.

Elephant, Horse, and Cow 1914

Tiger 1912

Here, Marc has kept the tiger's basic shape and colour, but made it simpler and brighter with angled edges – it almost looks like a big jewel sitting in a landscape of other precious stones.

Toward the end of his life, Marc's animals were almost getting lost among his brilliant colours and broken shapes. He took this style further and further until almost nothing in his work looked realistic.

Klee colour

German artist **PAUL KLEE** (pronounced "clay") (1879–1940) was one of the leading painters of the 20th century. His paintings are lively, colourful, and witty.

Can you find me in the painting?

The colourful Klee

Klee loved, studied, and wrote about colour. He began his career working in black and white. However, in 1914 he visited north Africa, and the bright sunlight awoke him to the beauty of colour.

"The beholder's eye, which moves like an animal grazing, follows paths prepared for it in the picture." PAUL KLEE

Painting with scissors

Landscape With Yellow Birds started off as a different piece of art. The orange-brown trees on the left and right edges of the picture used to be one tree. Klee wasn't happy with how the painting looked, so he cut it in half and reassembled it. Klee then left a strip between the two halves and painted two yellow birds poking out of the gap.

Klee kept things looking simple, as if a child had painted the art. However, this simple look was thoroughly planned and delicately carried out.

50

Landscape With Yellow Birds
By Paul Klee, **1923**
watercolour

The painting is this
big!

Artist

1923 // 32 Landschaft mit gelben Vögeln

STENCIL BIRDS

old plastic folders

You will need:
Old plastic folders
Marker pens
Scissors
Black card
Acrylic paints
Bits of sponge
Paint brushes
Old rubbers
Cup of water

Make sure you use thick paper or card.

1 On the old plastic folders, use the marker pen to draw some scenery shapes, such as trees and plants. You can use Klee's *Landscape With Yellow Birds* for inspiration.

2 Make your stencils by carefully cutting out the inside of the shapes, making sure you don't cut outside the line. Lightly sponge shades of blue across the top of the card for the sky.

3 Position your stencil over the black card and tape it in place along the top. Using a clean sponge, dab the paint over your stencil.

4 Now add some different colours. Lift the stencil and check your progress from time to time. Once finished, carefully remove the stencil.

5 Use the other stencils to create your landscape. Use masking tape to hold the stencil in place. Use a range of colours for the different shapes.

6 You can use your stencils as many times as you want. Try rotating them, or you can use different colours.

7 You are now ready to make your birds. Draw a bird body on one pencil rubber and a bird head on another, then carefully cut them out.

8 Use the rubber body and head as stamps. Dip them into yellow paint and then pick a place on your landscape and press down hard.

9 Once you have added all the yelllow birds you want, you can use a paint brush to add extra detail, such as feet, eyes, and wings.

10 As a finishing touch, use a fine paint brush to add detail to the plants and background. Use stripes and spots to break up flat colours.

FANCY FLYERS

From fat owls to graceful doves, birds appeal to artists of every kind.

Water-bird mosaic 4th century

Mosaics are pictures made by setting glass or marble chips into wet plaster. This mosaic is from an ancient empire and was found in Germany.

The Owl 1947

Pablo Picasso was inspired by the things around him, and he made several paintings of this injured owl perched on a wooden chair.

Birds c1959

Andy Warhol created this early ink drawing in the bright, clear colours he used for advertising artwork. Do you think it's about Christmas – partridges in a pear tree?

This duck family was carved by Inuits in the Arctic.

Man in a Bowler Hat 1935

For René Magritte, this bowler-hatted figure represented the common man – he painted lots of them, but he always covered the face to hide individual features. Experts think the dove symbolizes the human spirit.

Blue-Necked Bird 2002

Nancy Nicholson made this bird out of bits of stuck-on paper. A picture like this is called a "collage".

Eagle 2001

Ex-welder Joe Pogan makes sculptures out of reclaimed materials, which artists call "found" objects.

Three Studies of a Bullfinch c1505

The photographic detail and formal layout of this stunning watercolour by Albrecht Dürer make it look strangely modern.

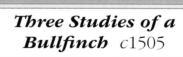

Pogan constructed his big eagle (it's 66cm/26in high) out of nuts and bolts, tools, cutlery, tokens, and brass buttons.

Fish and shapes

Spanish artist **PABLO PICASSO** (1881–1973) started creating artwork when he was just a child. Picasso was the most famous artist of the 20th century. He made sculptures, prints, and ceramics, as well as paintings.

The Soles
By Pablo Picasso **1940,**
Oil paint on canvas

The painting is this big!

Artist

Legendary artist

Picasso achieved fame in his own lifetime, unlike some of the other great artists. He co-founded Cubism with fellow artist Georges Braque. They broke up the shapes of objects and then re-arranged them decoratively on the canvas.

"*Everyone wants to understand painting. Why is there no attempt to understand the song of birds?*"

PABLO PICASSO

Colourful crabs

The Soles was painted by Picasso while he lived in Paris, France. He took inspiration from a small town on the French coast called Royan. Although the artwork is called *The Soles*, the fish in the painting aren't soles, and the crab is the most stand-out feature.

The crab shows how Picasso would simplify shapes and colours to give them more impact. It stands out clearly against the flat background.

The orange crab and its large claws reflect and balance the shape and colour of the measuring scales on the left.

CRAB COLLAGE

1 Cut and rip your magazine pages into small shapes. Start the collage background by using the blue scraps. Glue them onto your cardboard.

2 Gradually build you background with different tones of blue and try to create curves and bands of shape and colour.

Let's draw a crab

Break down the real shape of a crab into simple shapes. Try to use triangles, half circles, and rectangles. Then cut these out of the magazines.

body

claws

3 Position your crab shape and glue it on the collage. You can also add a few fish. Try matching them to the curves and shapes of the background.

MASTER'S ANIMALS

Here are a few animal-inspired pieces from the legendary artist, Picasso.

The Bull Man Drinking 1958

Picasso used animals and humans as subjects. He also used the half-man, half-bull Minotaur (from Greek mythology) in his paintings.

The Cock 1943

This painting shows how Picasso would break down a image into simple shapes and colour, without losing the identity of the image; you can still see it's a cockerel.

The Bullfight 1934

Bullfights are a traditional pastime in Spain and Picasso painted dozens of pictures showing the fights' drama and action.

Picasso painted in many different styles during his long career. In the 1930s he was influenced by the strangeness of surrealism, but he still captured the realities of life, as in _Cat Seizing a Bird_.

From the 1940s, Picasso started to turn his artistic talents to making ceramics. The _Wood-Owl_ is actually a painted ceramic jug.

Picasso often used scrap materials in his sculptures. The ribs of the goat were made from a wicker basket. It was covered in plaster and then cast in bronze.

She-Goat 1950

Wood-Owl 1968

Cool cats

BEFORE HE BECAME A FAMOUS pop artist in the 1960s, Andy Warhol (1928-1987) was an illustrator. He loved cats, and in 1954 he published a limited-edition book of drawings called *25 Cats Name Sam and One Blue Pussy*.

25 Cats Name Sam and One Blue Pussy
by Andy Warhol, **1954**,
hand-coloured lithographs

Each print is this
big!

Silly numbers

Despite its title, Warhol's book contains only these 16 cats called Sam. (Can you find one with a baby Sam?). There are no words apart from labels, done by Warhol's mother. When she was working on the cover, she wrote the title as "25 Cats Name Sam..." instead of "25 Cats Named Sam...". Warhol really liked random mistakes, though – in drawing and in writing – so he left the title that way.

"I never wanted to be a painter. I wanted to be a tap dancer." ANDY WARHOL

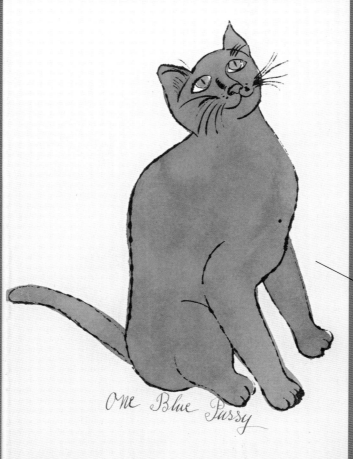

Warhol admired the work of American wildlife photographer Walter Chandoha, and owned a book of his cat images. Many of these drawings seem to be inspired by Chandoha's work, as well as by the painter's pets.

Experts think that *One Blue Pussy* is a portrait of one of Warhol's favourite cats, who had recently died. She was called Hester.

INKY DOGS

You will need:

Thick paper
Pencil
Pencil rubber
Black marker pen
Watercolour inks
Paint brush

Concentrated inks

Tip:
You only need to add a few drops of ink into a mixing tray, then dilute with water. Remember to test your colour on scrap paper before you start painting.

A mixing pallet helps to keep your colours separate.

Draw a Dog

Rather than trying to copy Andy Warhol's cats, why not try the same approach with a dog? The outline of a dog is easy to draw if you divide it into simple shapes.

Start with the dog's body. See how it gradually widens to from the tail to the ribcage. Now add block shapes for the neck and head.

Finally, add circles for the hips, shoulders, and head. Then straight lines for the legs and feet.

1 Before you start, it's a good idea to practise drawing the shape of your dog on scrap paper.

2 When you are ready, draw a pencil outline of your dog on the thick paper. Then go over your outline with a black marker pen and rub out the pencil lines.

3 With the black marker, roughen the outline and add more detail, such as spots, a collar, ears, a nose, and eyes.

5 Your finished dog should look simple and bold. You can add a little friend for your dog or try some other animals if you have time.

4 Choose an ink colour and fill inside the outline, or get a friend to help. (Warhol held drawing parties and at one, his guests, each coloured in a cat).

WILD IDEAS

Warhol is famous for film stars and soup tins, but he also cared about animals.

Grevy's zebra

Danger ahead

It was at the very start of his career, before he became famous, that Andy Warhol drew a collection of charming cats for his friends and family (see pages 64–65). But at the end of his life he turned his attention to different kinds of animal – those that have almost disappeared from the Earth. In 1983, Warhol produced ten powerful screenprints, each portraying one creature – all the pictures shown here come from this series, which is called *Endangered Species*. In 1986, the year before he died, he published 16 more screenprints of similar subjects in a book called *Vanishing Animals*.

Orangutan

To highlight these animals, Warhol used the same kind of harsh, artificial colours that made his pop-art portraits so striking.

Bald eagle

Bighorn ram

Animals for all

ANDY SCOTT (b 1964) makes public art. His enormous animals are found all over the world – always in places where lots of people can see them.

This beast, called *Ginger*, was inspired by a dray horse who lived near the artist's home. Dray horses are powerful animals that pull carts.

These sculptures are beautiful, but they still involve the same heavy cutting and welding as industrial metalwork.

Woven steel

All Scott's works are made of steel. First he builds a sturdy frame, then he welds onto it small sections of steel bar, which look almost like weaving. He then adds small lengths of steel in different shapes and diameters, depending on the size of the sculpture and how delicate each section will be. To make eyelashes, for example, he fits tiny, narrow pieces.

"So many artists have portrayed animals – I love using hard materials to give them character and movement."
ANDY SCOTT

The real story

Installed outside a veterinary clinic in South Australia, this work – *Loaded Dog* – illustrates a short story by Henry Lawson. In it, a dog called Tommy loves to play fetch, but he gets into trouble when, instead of a piece of wood, he fetches a stick of dynamite.

Heavy Horse
by Andy Scott, **1997,**
galvanised steel

The sculpture is
this **big!**

Artist

This Clydesdale horse,
Scott's first major
work, stands 4.5m (15ft)
tall overlooking a major
motorway in Scotland.

MONKEY ON A WIRE

You will need:

Pencil and paper
Cardboard
Pen and sticky tack
Garden wire and pliers
Masking tape
Paints

You can use spray
or acrylic paint.

Be very careful when using the wire.
If you need help always ask an adult.

1 Sketch out the shape of your monkey. Plan the frame of the body. You can copy a monkey from a book and break it down into simple shapes.

2 Use a pen to pierce a hole in the card (position the sticky tack underneath). Feed the end of the wire through the hole and tape it, as shown.

3 Start with the monkey's spine. Create a curved loop in the wire. It's easier to use long pieces of wire, remember to be careful of the sharp ends.

4 From the spine you can form the monkey's legs and feet. If you need use a new piece of wire, use pliers t hook it around the bottom of the spine.

5 Sculpt the basic shape of your monkey. From the legs you can add the tail. From the spine you can create the monkey's body and arms.

6 Create the head by sculpting several vertical circles and then one horizon circle around the middle. Use small pieces of wire to add the ear shapes.

Giraffe

Why not try different animals, such as a tall giraffe or a tiny mouse!

7 Start winding wire around the basic monkey frame. Around the body start with a criss-cross pattern and don't pull the wire too tight.

8 Wind the wire around the arms and legs. If you are finding it tricky, you can use the pliers. Finally, wind the wire around the head.

You can also paint the base.

9 As a finishing touch you can paint your sculpture silver. If you are using spray paints you must ask an adult to do it for you and they must use the paint outside where it is well ventilated.

Before   After

Bend the arms and hook the fingers so your monkey can hold on to things.

Mouse

Remember to make sure any sharp ends are bent inside the model!

Monkey

The tail can be delicate so be careful when you paint and display your model!

75

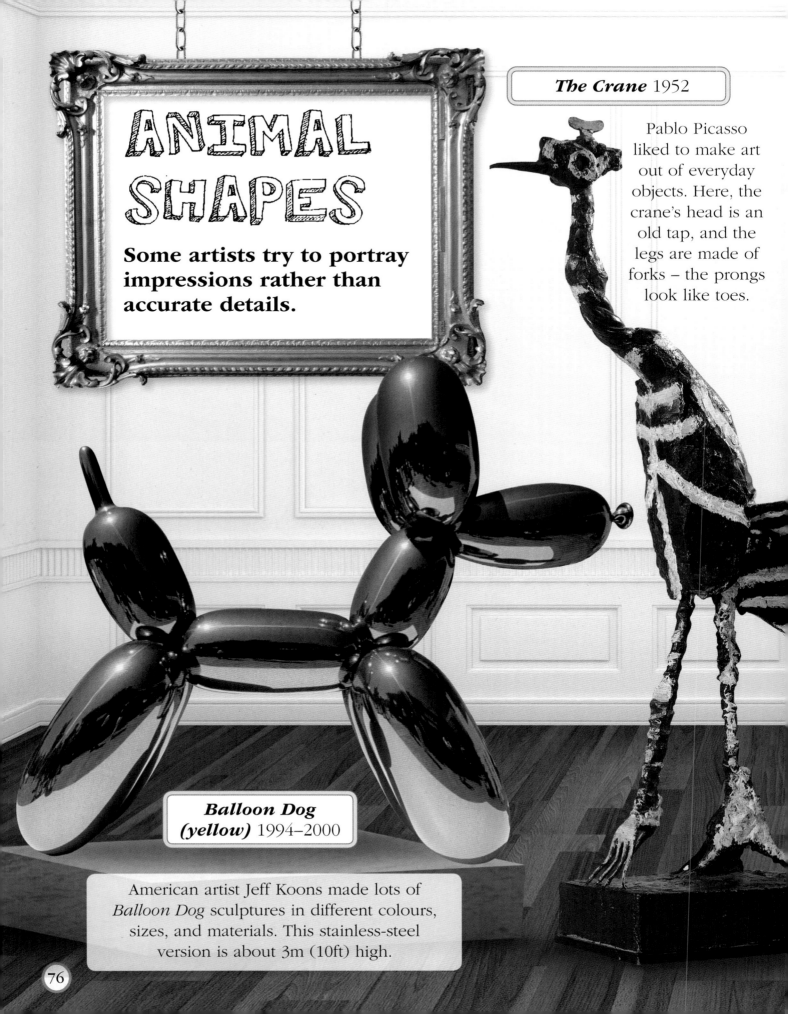

ANIMAL SHAPES

Some artists try to portray impressions rather than accurate details.

The Crane 1952

Pablo Picasso liked to make art out of everyday objects. Here, the crane's head is an old tap, and the legs are made of forks – the prongs look like toes.

Balloon Dog (yellow) 1994–2000

American artist Jeff Koons made lots of *Balloon Dog* sculptures in different colours, sizes, and materials. This stainless-steel version is about 3m (10ft) high.

Head of a Bull 1943

Picasso needed only two bits of an old bicycle to make this bull's head – the handlebars are the horns, and the seat is the head.

Beast Alerted 1990

Using his skills as a metal-worker as well as an artist, Lynn Chadwick tried to show how animals feel. Does this bronze creature look peaceful or panicky to you?

Mammoth 2008

In the California desert, Mexican-American sculptor Ricardo Breceda has created a herd of life-size prehistoric beasts. Most of his figures, like this mammoth (early elephant), are made in sheet metal with recycled bits added on.

Bird 1959

Henry Moore was inspired to create this bronze figure by watching an injured crow that came to drink at his bird table.

Glossary

acrylic paint
A type of paint popular since the 1950s. It looks like oil paint, but it's mixed with water and dries more quickly.

canvas
A cloth that artists paint on, usually made of linen or cotton.

collage
A picture made by sticking assorted materials to paper or board.

engraving
A print made from a block that has a design cut or carved on it.

Expressionism
A style of painting where the artist shows emotions and feelings by painting distorted or exaggerated objects rather than realistic ones.

fresco
A painting done in watercolour onto wet plaster. The paint sinks into the plaster as it dries.

gouache
Watercolour paint mixed with a special glue-like substance.

hieroglyphs
A small picture of an object that represents a word, sound, or idea.

lithograph
A print in which the design is drawn with a greasy crayon onto a slab of special stone.

mask
A face covering that hides people's identity, or helps them look like something or someone else.

mosaic
A picture or pattern made up of thousands of tiny pieces, usually of glass or stone.

oil paint
Paint in which the colours are mixed with sticky oils from plants or other sources. It is a favourite with artists as it can create many different effects.

pastel
A stick of dried paint made from powdered colour. It is like a crayon, but not greasy.

pattern
A decorative design.

pigment
Powdered colour mixed with liquid to make paint.

Pop art
A type of art that uses bold images like those in comics or advertising.

portrait
A picture or sculpture of a person, especially the face.

screenprint
A print made by wiping ink through a silk mesh onto paper or canvas. Parts of the mesh block the ink to make the design.

sculpture
Art made in three dimensions, usually from materials such as stone, wood, metal, or plastic.

sketch
A rough drawing that acts as a plan for a piece of art.

symbol
A sign or object that stands for something else. For example, lions in paintings may be used to represent royalty.

texture
The look and feel of the surface of a material.

watercolour
A type of paint in which solid colours are mixed with water, then applied with a brush.

woodblock print
A print made from a design that has been carved onto a block of wood. A different wood block is used for each colour required.

Index

acrylic paints 52
Africa 43, 50
afterlife 6, 13
Ancient Egyptian 6–7, 12–13
Asia 19
Australia 70
baboon 12
Becker do Valle, Rosina 42
Belgium 21
birds 18, 50, 52–55, 56, 57, 63, 77
Bloomfield, Frances Anne 42
Brazil 42
Breceda, Ricardo 77
bull 45, 62, 77
bullfight 62
cat 7, 13, 49, 63, 64–65
cattle 6
Chadwick, Lynn 77
chalks 21, 22, 30–31
Chandoha, Walter 65
cheetah 32
cockerel 62
collage 57, 60–61
colours 45
cow 49
crab 59, 60–61
crane 76
cubism 59
deer 19
dog 49, 66–67, 70
dove 57
ducks 56
Dürer, Albrecht 14–15, 17, 18–19, 57
eagle 57, 69
Egypt 7
elephant 46–47, 49, 69
Europe 14, 19, 21
Expressionist 44–45
falcon 13
fish 59
fishing 12
foil 8, 16–17
fox 48, 49
France 26, 59
fresco 6–7

geese 12
Germany 19, 21, 56
giraffe 74
goat 63
gouache 19
hare 18
Hawkins, William L 42
hieroglyphs 6, 11
horse 27, 28–29, 32, 33, 48, 49, 70–71
human body 7
ink drawing 56, 66–67
Inuits 56
Kidd, Odile 43
Klee, Paul 50–51,
Koons, Jeff 76
India 32, 34
lion 7, 20–21, 22–25, 26, 28–29
lithograph 65
Magritte, René 57
mammoth 77
man 35, 39–41, 57
Marc, Franz 44–45
mask 22–25
Minotaur 62
monkey 19, 33, 72–75
Moore, Henry 77
mosaic 56
mouse 26, 74
Nicholson, Nancy 57
oil painting 20–21, 28–29, 58–59
orangutan 68
organ 35
origami 43
owl 18, 56, 63
oxen 13
parrot 27
pastels 8–11, 30–31
Picasso, Pablo 56, 58–59, 62, 76
plants 46–47
plaster 8–11
Pogan, Joe 57
pop art 68–69
ram 69
rats 7
Renaissance 15

rhinoceros 14–15
Rousseau, Henri 42
Rubens, Peter Paul 20–21, 26–27
Scotland 71
Scott, Andy 70–71
screenprints 68–69
sculpture 21, 57, 63, 70–71, 76–77
snakes 7
Snyders, Frans 26
spaniel 32
squirrels 19
stag 32
steel 70–71
stencils 52–55
Stubbs, George 28–29, 32–33
tiger 27, 36–41, 42–43
Tipu Sultan 34
tomb 6, 11, 12–13
tortoise 16–17
toy 34–35
Toyei, Kiuho 43
trees 46–47, 50, 52–55
wall painting *see* fresco
Warhol, Andy 56, 64–65
watercolour 19, 46–47, 57
wax crayons 46–47
wire 72–75
woodcut 14–15
zebra 33, 68

Acknowledgements

Dorling Kindersley would like to thank the following for their kind permission to reproduce their photographs:
(Key: a-above; b-below/bottom; c-centre; f-far; l-left; r-right; t-top)

2 The Trustees of the British Museum: (t). **Corbis:** The Print Collector (b). **3 The Bridgeman Art Library:** Pushkin Museum, Moscow, Russia/Giraudon (br); Walker Art Gallery, National Museums Liverpool (tl). **V&A Images/Victoria and Albert Museum, London:** (tr). **4 Artothek:** Private Collection. Photo Hans Hinz (cl). **The Bridgeman Art Library:** Scottish National Gallery of Modern Art, Edinburgh, UK/© Succession Picasso/DACS, London 2011. (tl). **Andy Scott:** Hanneke van Wel (br). **Sotheby's, Inc., New York:** © 2011 The Andy Warhol Foundation for the Visual Arts/ARS, NY/DACS, London (tr). **6 The Trustees of the British Museum. 7 Alamy Images:** Ivy Close Images (t). **Corbis:** Bojan Brecelj (c, br). **12-13 Fotolia:** arquiplay77 (background). **12 The Art Archive:** Gianni Dagli Orti (bl). **Getty Images:** DEA/G. Dagli Orti (tr). **Photo Scala, Florence:** Egyptian Museum, Cairo (br). **13 The Art Archive:** Gianni Dagli Orti (tl). **The Bridgeman Art Library:** Ancient Art and Architecture Collection Ltd. (bl). **Getty Images:** De Agostini (r). **14 Corbis:** The Print Collector. **14-15 Corbis:** The Print Collector (t). **15 Alamy Images:** Interfoto (tl, b). **Corbis:** The Print Collector (crb). **Fotolia:** Carlos Caetano (cr). **18-19 Fotolia:** arquiplay77 (background). **18 akg-images:** Erich Lessing (l). **Getty Images:** (tr); **The Bridgeman Art Library** (br). **19 akg-images:** Joseph Martin (br). **Alamy Images:** The Art Gallery Collection (tr). **Getty Images:** The Bridgeman Art Library (tl). **21 The Trustees of the British Museum:** (br). **Getty Images:** (bl). **TopFoto.co.uk:** Fine Art Images/Heritage Images (tr). **26 akg-images:** Erich Lessing (tr). **The Bridgeman Art Library:** By Kind Permission of the Chequers Trust/Mark Fiennes (br, bl). **27 akg-images:** Electa (br). **The Bridgeman Art Library:** Samuel Courtauld Trust, The Courtauld Gallery, London, UK (bl). **Photo Scala, Florence:** © 2011. White Images (t). **28 The Bridgeman Art Library:** The British Sporting Art Trust (bl); Walker Art Gallery, National Museums Liverpool (c, tl). **29 The Bridgeman Art Library:** Walker Art Gallery, National Museums Liverpool. **30 The Bridgeman Art Library:** Walker Art Gallery, National Museums Liverpool (tr). **32-33 Fotolia:** arquiplay77 (background). **32 The Bridgeman

Art Library:** Manchester Art Gallery, UK (l); Private Collection (t); Yale Center for British Art, Gift of Paul Mellon, USA (br). **33 The Bridgeman Art Library:** National Gallery, London, UK. (tl); Yale Center for British Art, Paul Mellon Collection, USA (bl); Private Collection (r). **34-35 V&A Images/Victoria and Albert Museum, London:** (tl, b, tr). **42-43 Fotolia:** arquiplay77 (background). **42 The Bridgeman Art Library:** Frances Broomfield/Portal Gallery, London (br). **Corbis:** Images.com/Ricco/Maresca Gallery, New York (tr). **43 The Bridgeman Art Library:** Private Collection (tl). **Corbis:** The Print Collector (tr). **Gertrud Kanu:** LAVA, Laboratory for Visionary Architecture (br). **LAVA, Laboratory for Visionary Architecture, www.l-a-v-a.net:** Patrick Bingham Hall (cl). **44 The Bridgeman Art Library:** Pushkin Museum, Moscow, Russia/Giraudon. **45 akg-images:** (tl). **The Bridgeman Art Library:** Pushkin Museum, Moscow, Russia/Giraudon (cr). **Corbis:** Alexander Burkatovski (br). **48 Alamy Images:** Albert Knapp (l). **The Bridgeman Art Library:** Van der Heydt Museum, Wuppertal, Germany (br). **Corbis:** The Gallery Collection (t). **48-49 Fotolia:** arquiplay77 (background). **49 The Bridgeman Art Library:** Kunsthalle, Mannheim, Germany/Interfoto (t); Stadtische Galerie im Lenbachhaus, Munich, Germany/Interfoto (r); Private Collection (bl). **50-51 Artothek:** Private Collection. Photo Hans Hinz. **52 Artothek:** Private Collection. Photo Hans Hinz (br). **56-57 Fotolia:** arquiplay77 (background). **56 The Bridgeman Art Library:** The Israel Museum, Jerusalem, Israel/Gift of the Artist/© Succession Picasso/DACS, London 2011 (cl); Private Collection/Photo © Boltin Picture Library (bl). **Corbis:** © 2011 The Andy Warhol Foundation for the Visual Arts/ARS, NY/DACS, London (br); Alfredo Dagli Orti/The Art Archive (t). **57 The Bridgeman Art Library:** Private Collection/© ADAGP, Paris and DACS, London 2011 (tl); Real Monasterio de El Escorial, El Escorial, Spain (br). **Corbis:** Jacqui Hurst (tr). **Joe Pogan:** Photo Willy Paul (bl). **58 The Bridgeman Art Library:** Scottish National Gallery of Modern Art, Edinburgh, UK/© Succession Picasso/DACS,

London 2011. **59 akg-images:** ullstein bild (tc). **62-63 Fotolia:** arquiplay77 (background). **62 The Bridgeman Art Library:** Private Collection/James Goodman Gallery, New York, USA/© Succession Picasso/DACS, London 2011 (bl). **Getty Images:** Superstock/© Succession Picasso/DACS, London 2011 (br). **Photo Scala, Florence:** Mougins, Picasso Collection/© Succession Picasso/DACS, London 2011 (t). **63 Alamy Images:** Lamb (bl/pedestal). **Christie's:** © Succession Picasso/DACS, London 2011 (bl). **Corbis:** The Gallery Collection/© Succession Picasso/DACS, London 2011 (t). **Photo Scala, Florence:** © 2011 Digital image, The Museum of Modern Art, New York/© Succession Picasso/DACS, London 2011(br). **64-65 Sotheby's, Inc.:** 2011 Tobias Meyer, principal auctioneer, #9588677 © 2011 The Andy Warhol Foundation for the Visual Arts/ARS, NY/DACS, London. **66 S. Moore Photography:** (br). **67 S. Moore Photography:** (tl, tr, bl, cr). **68 Corbis:** © 2011 The Andy Warhol Foundation for the Visual Arts/ARS, NY/DACS, London. Courtesy Ronald Feldman Fine Arts, New York/www.feldmangallery.com (tr, br). **69 Corbis:** © 2011 The Andy Warhol Foundation for the Visual Arts/ARS, NY/DACS, London. Courtesy Ronald Feldman Fine Arts, New York/www.feldmangallery.com/© DACS 2011 (bc, t, bl); **Rex Features:** Nils Jorgensen (br). **70 Andy Scott:** Caroline Scott (tl); Nisbet Wylie Photographs (tc); Hanneke van Wel (bl). **71 Andy Scott:** Hanneke van Wel. **76 Alamy Images:** Sandra Baker/Jeff Koons (l). **Photo Scala, Florence:** BPK, Bildagentur fuer Kunst, Kultur und Geschichte, Berlin/© Succession Picasso/DACS, London 2011 (r). **77 The Bridgeman Art Library:** Private Collection (tr). **Getty Images:** Courtesy Ricardo A Breceda (cr). **Photo Scala, Florence:** Reproduced by permission of The Henry Moore Foundation (br); © 2011. White Images/© Succession Picasso/DACS, London 2011 (tl) **Jacket images:** Front: Alamy Images: Albert Knapp bl.

All other images © Dorling Kindersley
For further information see: www.dkimages.com